E $7.45
Ar   Arvetis, Chris
               Why is the sky
           blue?

Why Is the Sky Blue?

A **Just Ask** Book

Hi, my name is Christopher

by Chris Arvetis
and Carole Palmer

illustrated by James Buckley

Copyright © 1986 by Rand McNally & Company
All rights reserved
Printed in Italy

Library of Congress Catalog Card Number: 85-63022

CHILDRENS PRESS CHOICE

A Rand McNally title selected for educational distribution

ISBN 0-516-09812-8

1986 SCHOOL AND LIBRARY EDITION

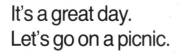

It's a great day.
Let's go on a picnic.

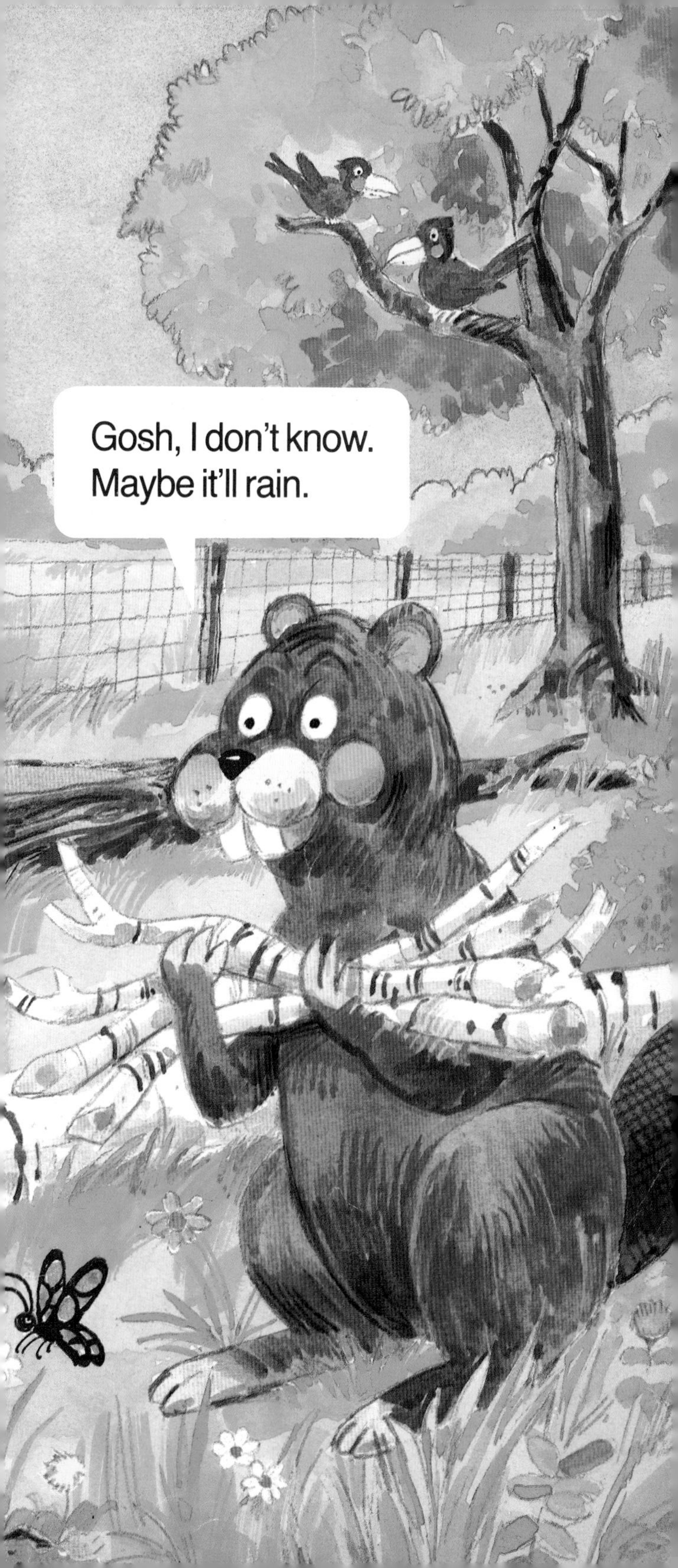
Gosh, I don't know. Maybe it'll rain.

But look at the sky
See how blue it is.
It probably won't
rain today.

Well, I guess you're right. The clear blue sky means it won't rain.

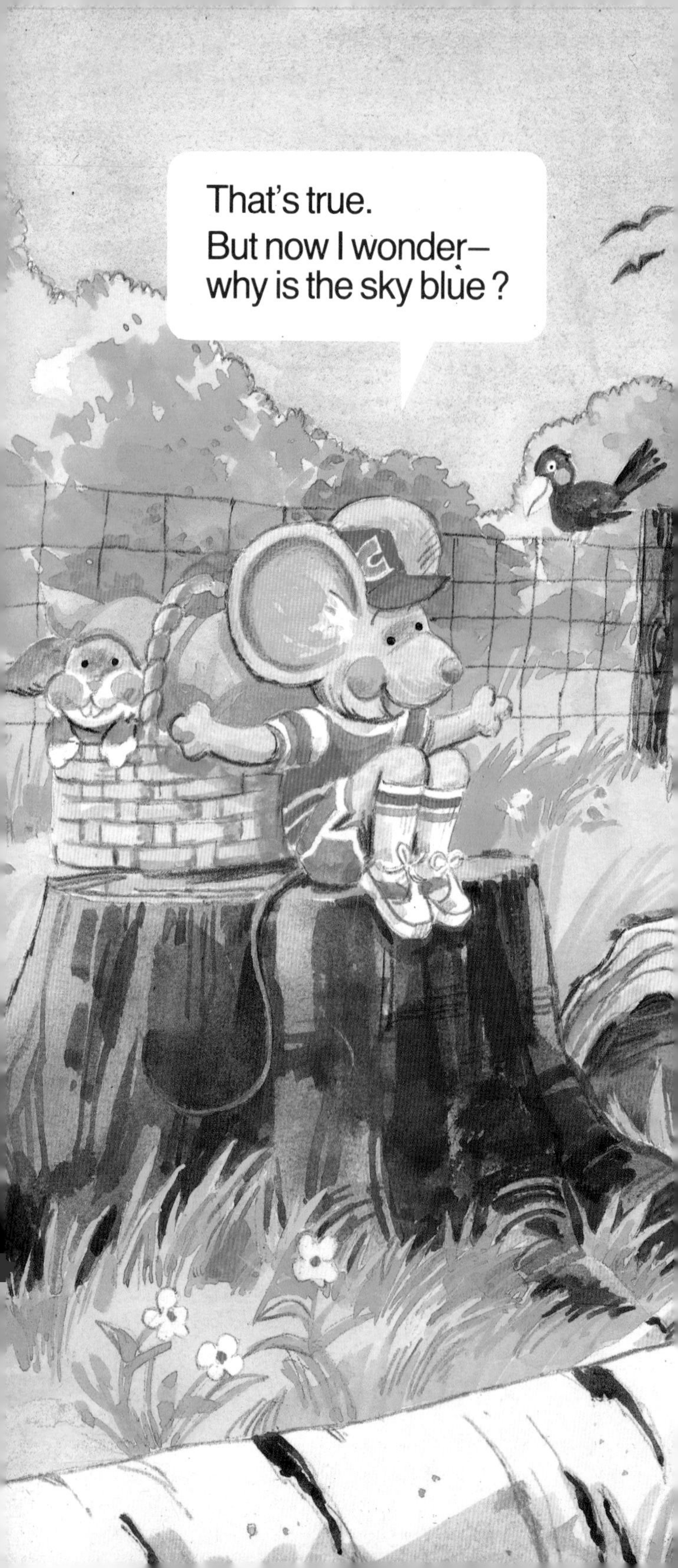
That's true.
But now I wonder–
why is the sky blue?

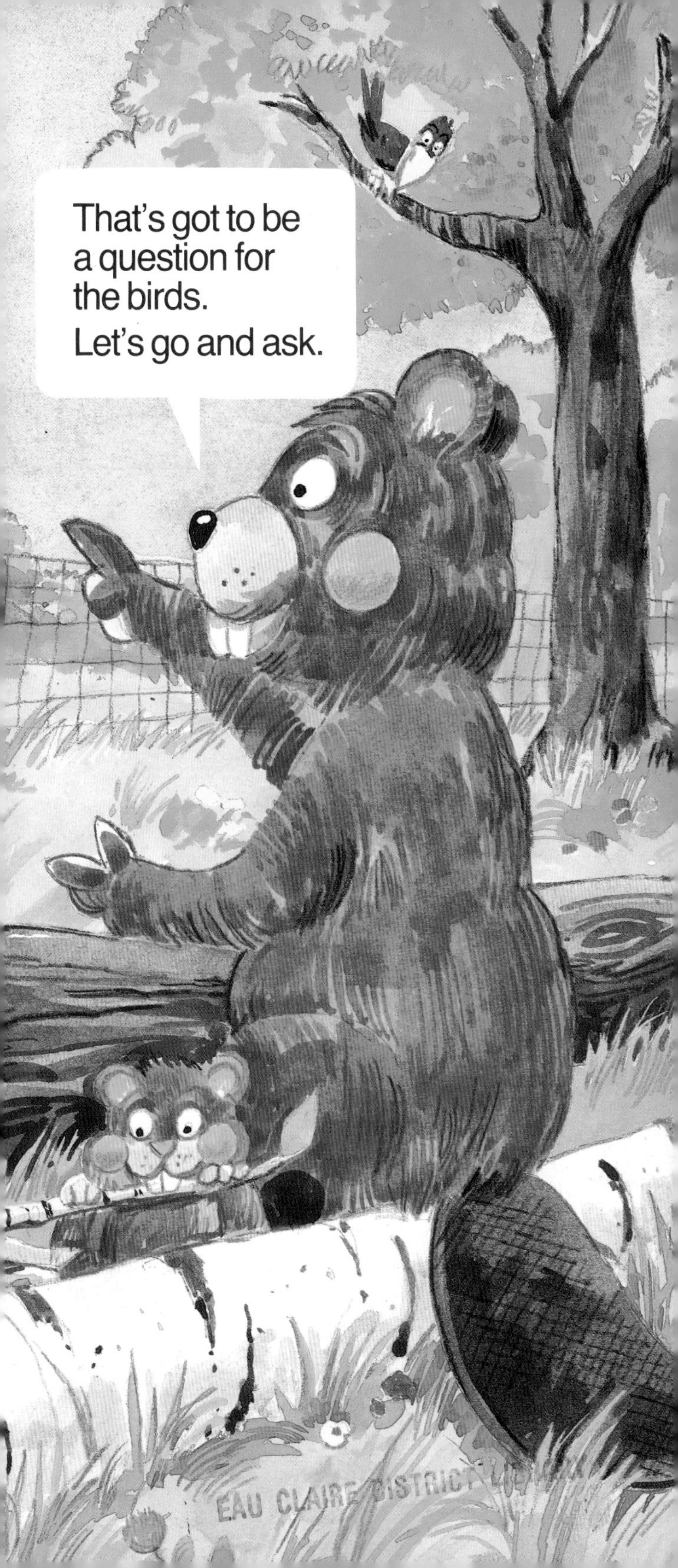
That's got to be a question for the birds.
Let's go and ask.

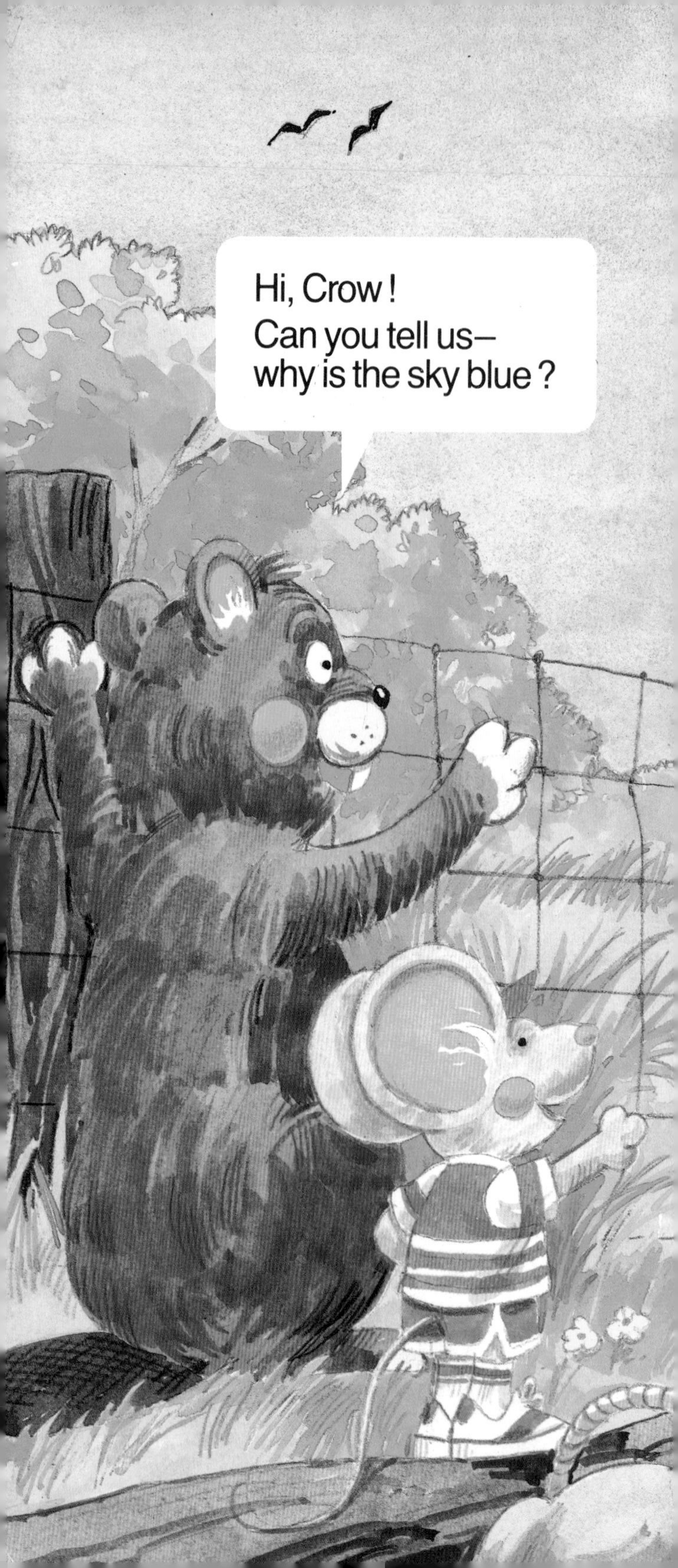
Hi, Crow!
Can you tell us–
why is the sky blue?

I'll try to answer, but that is a hard question.

First of all, you have to learn about the sky. Sky is a word we use to name all of the air above us.

It is the earth's ATMOSPHERE.

That's a big word!

Say it with me.

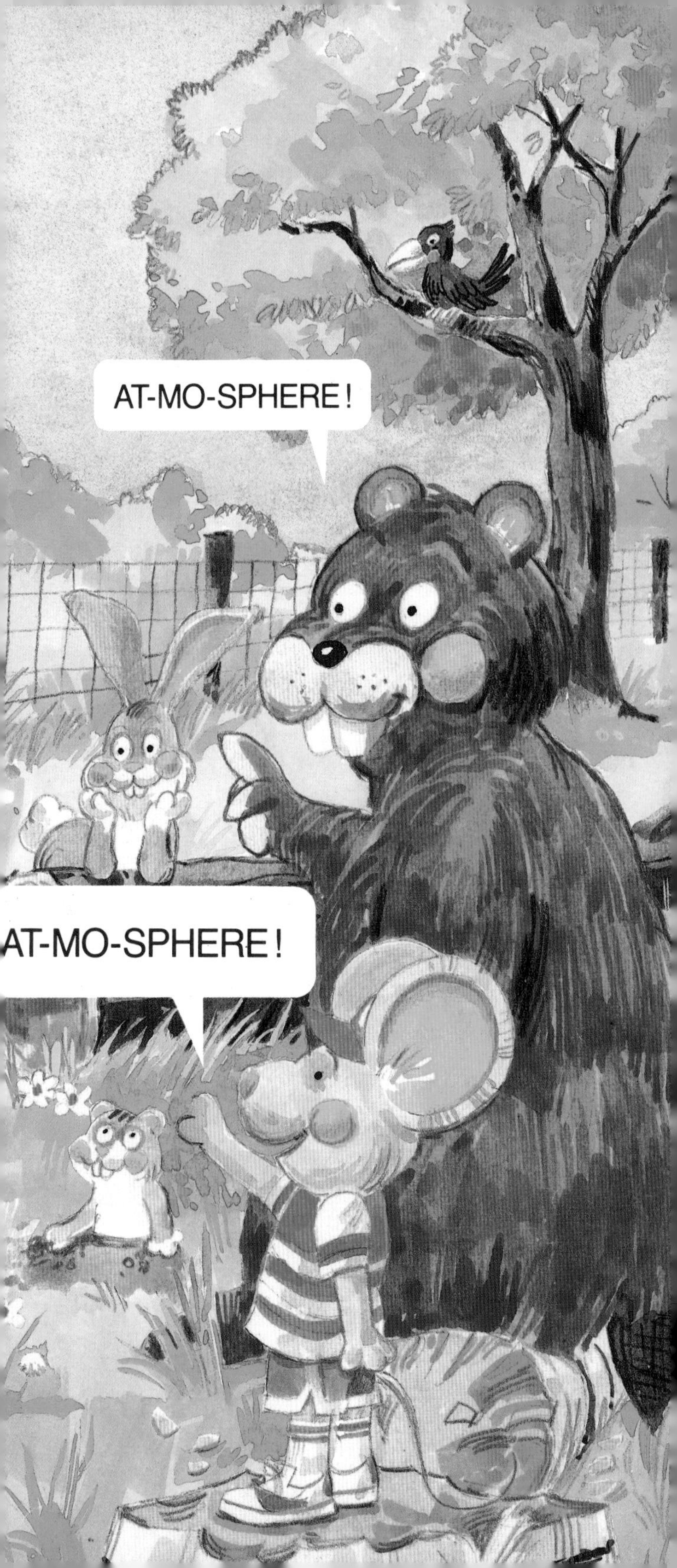
AT-MO-SPHERE!
AT-MO-SPHERE!

The earth's atmosphere is made up of many little parts called MOLECULES. That's another gigantic word— say MOL-E-CULES!

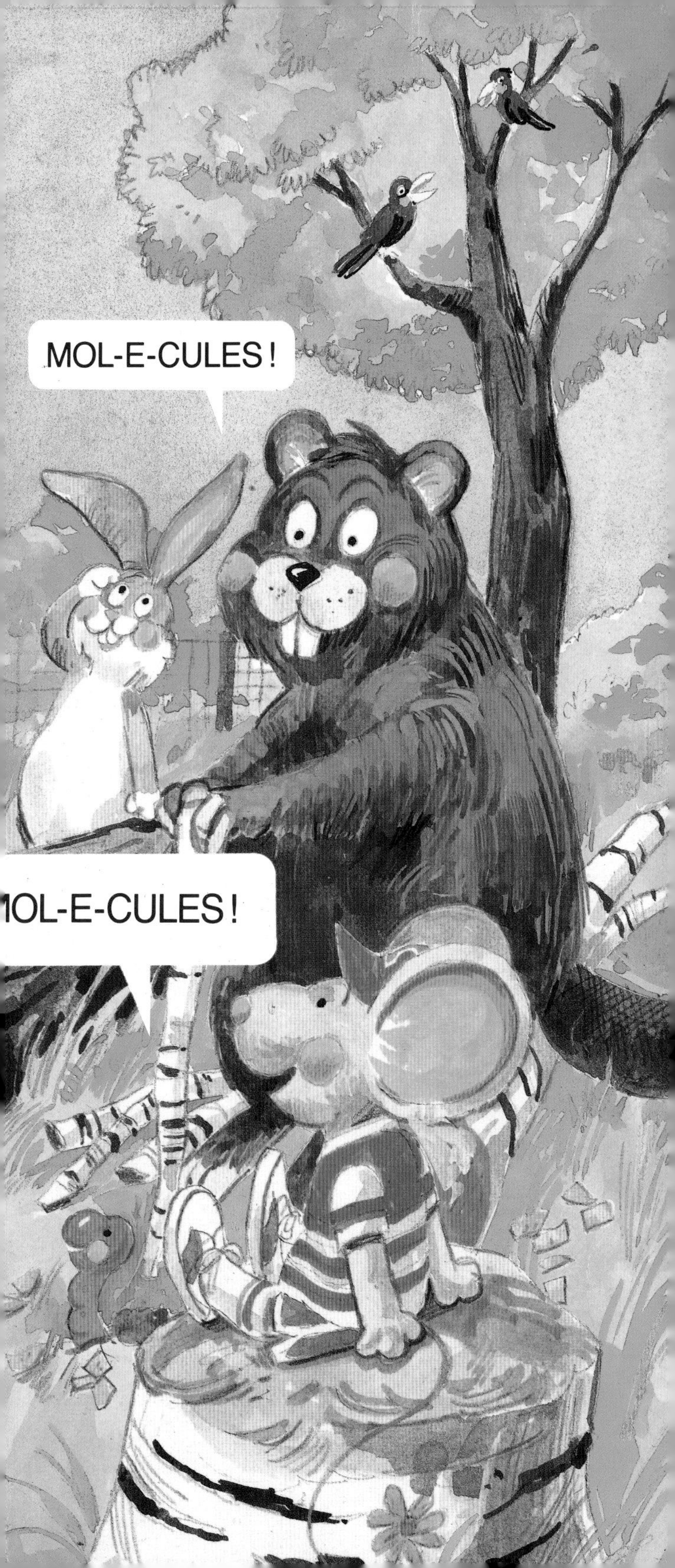
MOL-E-CULES!
OL-E-CULES!

The air is made up of many little molecules. We cannot see molecules, but we know they are there.

The light from the sun passes through these molecules. Let me draw you pictures to show what happens.

Sunlight is made up of many colors. If we could look inside a sun's ray, we would see violet, blue, green, yellow, orange, and red– a rainbow of colors.
Beautiful!

When the sunlight shines through the molecules in the atmosphere, the light is scattered in all directions. Look at what I mean.

The molecules scatter more blue light than any other color.
That is why the sky looks blue.
Fascinating !

When the sun rises and sets, a lot of blue light is lost. We see the red or pink colors. Those are the colors we see in the sky at sunrise and sunset.

On a very cloudy or rainy day, some of the light is stopped by all the clouds.

We see only the gray or milky white sky— no pretty colors.

And then there are days like today when we see some fluffy white clouds in the sky and the rest of the sky is very blue.

The color of the sky depends on how the light travels through the atmosphere. When it's a clear day, we see a beautiful blue sky.
I'm thirsty !

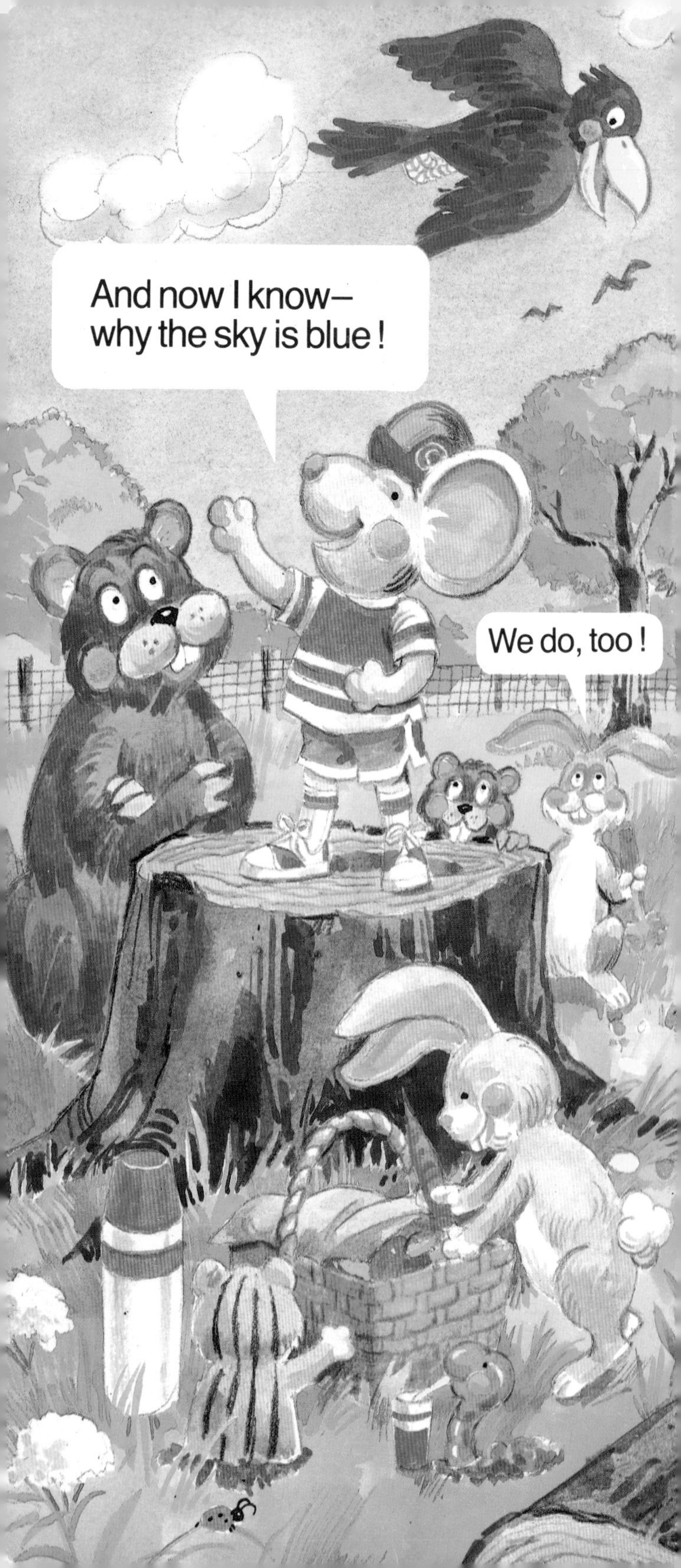
And now I know–
why the sky is blue!
We do, too!